The 20 Minute Financial Plan

How to Get Your Financial Plan Created and in Place in Just 20 Minutes

By Phil Randazzo, MBA

This book is presented solely for educational and entertainment purposes. The author and publisher are not offering it as legal, accounting, or other professional services advice. While best efforts have been used in preparing this book, the author and publisher make no representations or warranties of any kind and assume no liabilities of any kind with respect to the accuracy or completeness of the contents and specifically disclaim any implied warranties of merchantability or fitness of use for a particular purpose. Neither the author nor the publisher shall be held liable or responsible to any person or entity with respect to any loss or incidental or consequential damages caused, or alleged to have been caused, directly or indirectly, by the information or programs contained herein. Every company and idea is different, and the advice and strategies contained herein may not be suitable for your situation. You cannot rely on the materials in this book in making business or financial related decisions, and you should seek the services of competent professional professionals who are fully advised of all relevant facts pertinent to your situation before making any decision relating to launching, running, or selling any business.

Here's What's Inside...

Foreword

Las Vegas, NV
June 2014

One of the things people often ask me is how they can save for their future but still enjoy today. Today's lifestyle persuades you to live abundantly in the here and now, so I know how easy it is to put off planning for your retirement.

I've spent 22 plus years working with individuals and business owners. I've found that people spend more time planning a weekend vacation than they spend planning their future. I felt compelled to write this book, showing you how to have the best of both worlds - a great life today, but not at the expense of a great life when you retire.

I want to take the mystery out of saving for your retirement. It's not difficult, and this book will show you how this is true. In fact, I say you can do the planning in less time than it takes to drink a cup of coffee.

Enjoy the book!

I hope this book educates you on the successful retirement strategies you can utilize, and change your way of thinking about your future and encourages you to get started on your better future today.

My Best!

Introduction

Did you know the average person retires with only $1,000 in savings? Only about 28% of Americans are able to retire at a comfortable level. Clearly, advance planning is not taking place. The mindset is, "I want to live for today and don't know if tomorrow's going to happen." This is the paycheck-to-paycheck mindset. All of a sudden time creeps up on you and it's time to retire, or you are unable to work because of an illness or disability. Then the time for saving is gone. It is not hard to plan for the future.

I've heard so many excuses over the past 22 years. "As soon as I get a raise" is a popular one. "As soon as I pay off my car." Or "As soon as I pay off that credit card debt." I've heard excuse after excuse. There will never be a "good time" to start saving. You have to put those excuses aside. As soon as the car is paid off, guess what? You are going to go buy a new car and have another car payment. Or you will plan a vacation or buy a new TV. There are endless amounts of wants to tempt us in this world. As soon as the credit card is paid off, statistics show that 90% of people go back and recharge that credit card, unless they cut it up.

When I walk through the grocery store, I have to avoid the cookie aisle because I know my willpower is just not there. I'm going to buy the cookies and eat them if I do. With savings, you have to set it up automatically and just start, otherwise you go down the cookie aisle and get distracted! There will never be a good time to start saving for retirement, college planning, that lake cabin you want to buy, or whatever the case may be. You just need to start.

The good news is that in 20 minutes, you can set up a system, an automated system, and start saving for your future or any other financial goal. It doesn't require much discipline or willpower on your part and it's really simple.

Let me show you how.

Funds & Buckets™

It is important to have money allocated into automatic savings before you spend it. Most Americans see money in their bank account and decide how to empty it the quickest way they know how. I have created a system called Funds and Buckets™, which distributes your money as soon as you receive it to make life easier. Buckets are set up to achieve long term goals such as retirement, college, home, bills, etc. Some funds are specifically used for just having "Fun."

I had a client at my office yesterday whose mom just passed away and he had no idea how much money his mom had. She was completely frugal her whole life. She was a depression era child and had several hundred thousand dollars saved, but she lived so frugally that she wouldn't even subscribe to magazines because she wanted to save the $12 per year. Imagine making a few small sacrifices and having it equate to hundreds of thousands of dollars in the future!

The idea of saving goes against the very nature of living in a consumer-driven economy. I encourage people to save money, but also to reward themselves - to have fun! Because if all you do is save, save, save and there's no fun at the end, it's no fun, right? That's where people will say, "Oh, this isn't fun," and stop what they're doing. I encourage people to have that fun bucket, as it creates another bucket more valuable than anything in retirement - your memories bucket. That's something that is just so rewarding that will continue to motivate people throughout life and retirement.

By separating your money, you create multiple buckets that make life more enjoyable. Everyone has heard the saying "Don't put all your eggs in one basket." I say, 'Don't put all of your money into one bucket."

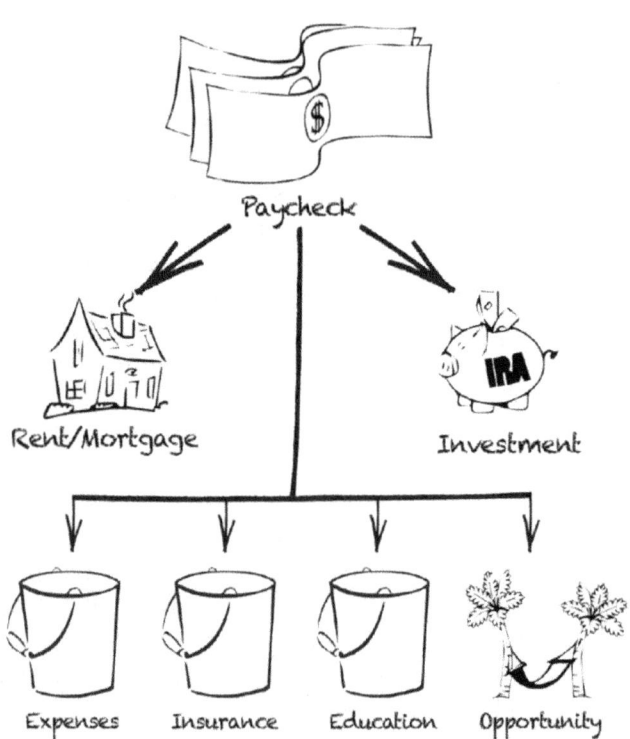

Mortgage – Bucket

Having a place to live is one of the most important things in life. The ultimate goal is to make sure you have a place to live, both right now and into retirement. Whether that is owning or renting your place to live, ultimately, you need to have a place that is 'yours'. If you can guarantee that the shelter you have is yours to keep, you will live a lot more comfortably.

If you do own your home, paying it off would be a great plan for your retirement. Imagine not having a mortgage payment. How else would you spend that money? Whether in retirement or before, having your home paid off is an amazing thing. If you can allocate additional money to this bucket and pay your mortgage twice a month instead of just once, you can significantly reduce the repayment time and decrease the overall interest paid.

If you rent your current place of living, preparing a budget for retirement that includes an increasing rent payment is key. Your current rent payment will increase over time. And don't fret, owning a home is not everyone's dream. Planning for both now and your future allows you to be prepared for anything that might come your way.

Investment – Bucket

Many financial advisers agree with Albert Einstein's adage that "Compound Interest" is the "Eighth wonder of the world". There is a huge power in growing your money slowly over time with proper investment. Never before in the history of our world have we been able to invest so easily in things that grow as we have today. Many companies offer a program called a 401k. Money can be taken out automatically at payday and deposited into an account that is designed to grow tax efficiently! Most people get frustrated and overwhelmed by the choices that are offered in these accounts. Little do they know that they are professionally managed choices that take out all the guesswork.

Hint: They're typically called target-dated funds, or Lifecycle Funds. These funds are set up to match your targeted retirement year to the kind of risk your account can withhold. You just have to sit back, save and let the money work for you.

The next big question is, "How much should you save?" Answer: "As much as you can!" I've never worked with anyone transitioning into retirement saying, "I wish I hadn't saved this much." Now, on the other hand, I have worked with many clients that say, "I wish I would have enjoyed myself more," or "I should have taken that trip," or "I shouldn't have worked so hard." With this being said, you have to invest and enjoy yourselves. At the end of the day, you can't take it with you. This is where a great planner comes in to make sure you're on track for your goals and still enjoying your life.

FACTS:
- Average 401k balance is $82,000.
- Rule of 72 - Divide your Rate of Return or interest rate - that's how long it takes to double your money. 72/8=9 years.
- Save $100 each paycheck, earn 8% and in 30 years it will equal $293,000.
- Waiting to start saving just five years requires more monthly investment to reach $500,000 by age 65, assuming 8% rate of return.

30 years of age - $283   35 years of age - $354   40 years of age - $550

Cost of Delayed Saving

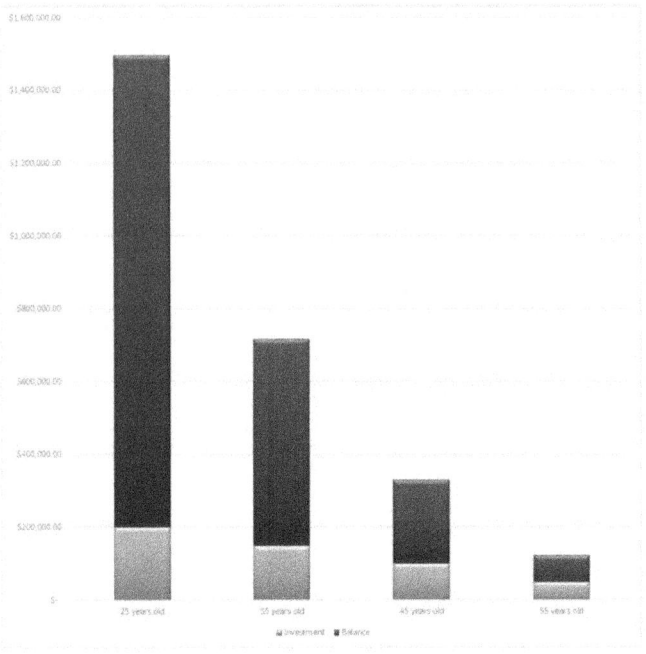

This graph shows the benefit of starting your retirement saving early. Each bar shows the age that the saver started investing $200 a month (at 8% interest). The lower section is the amount of money each individual invested. The dark, upper section is the amount of accrued interest each investor would have potentially earned due to compounding interest.

Benefits of Compounding Interest

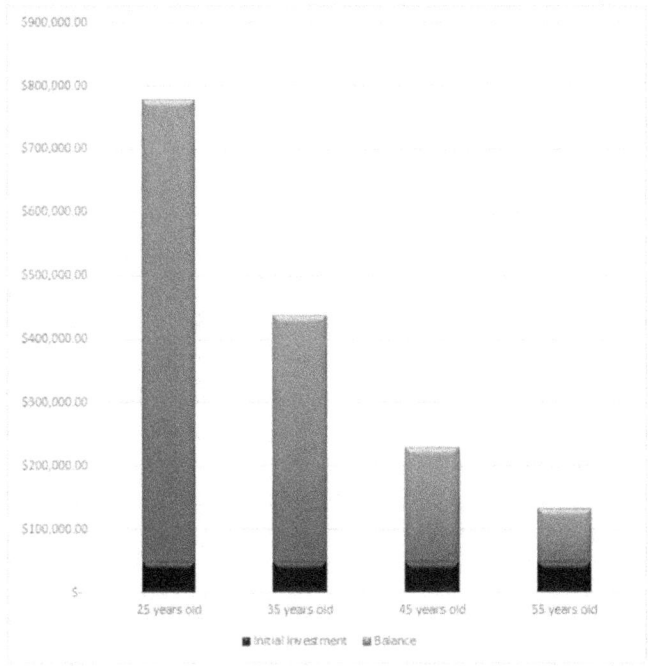

This graph shows four individuals who started saving at the age noted. Each invested $5,000 every year for ten years and then stopped saving. Not removing any money from the account, this is the amount of money each investor would have at age 65.

Expenses – Bucket

Expenses include utilities, groceries, debt payments, and other household needs. You can put these things into categories and give yourself limits on what you need to spend in each. You might find that besides your mortgage, this bucket is the biggest bucket. This bucket tends to have some of the biggest holes too. Most people keep pouring more and more money into it without having any paycheck left over for other buckets. The best way to make this bucket work is to reduce unnecessary spending.

There are great websites out there, like Mint.com, LearnVest.com, and CreditKarma.com, which allow you to categorize your expenses, creating an easy way to follow a budget. At the end of the month you can see where your money is going and discover where you are wasting it. You might find you are spending over $400 a month on eating out. You can then make the necessary changes to adjust your habits by possibly giving yourself a budget or making it a goal to only spend $350 the next month. Filling just the smallest of holes can make a big difference in what you put into your other buckets. You can do all of this on your own in a short period of time and even track it on your smartphone!

Insurance – Bucket

A good financial plan can be destroyed in seconds if you get hit with an unexpected, catastrophic loss. That's why it's important to create an insurance bucket to help protect against such losses. It is true that people can be over-insured. It is quite easy to insure everything in your life, so make sure you're not over-insured.

Some important types of insurance that we recommend are life, health, homeowners, car, and disability insurance. For immediate planning needs, term life can be quite inexpensive. Disability insurance helps protect your income if you can't work. Many of these might be offered through your employer. Critical point - make sure you have the right amount of life insurance! All too many times I've seen the surviving spouse struggling to survive because their loved one didn't have enough life insurance.

As you get closer to retirement, long-term care can be a huge strain on finances. Here in the U.S. we have 9,000 people a day turning age 65. At some point in their life, retirees are going to need some type of home health care or a long term care facility to go into. My dad spent time at a long-term care facility a couple of years before he passed away. My grandmother spent 11 years in a long-term care facility. The average cost for that was $6,500 a month in today's dollars.

Insurance can be an important part in making sure life doesn't take away from your goals. When we walk you through your 20 minute plan we will go over which ones might be best for you. Insurance never is one size fits all and many agents will try to over-insure you.

Education – Bucket

Most people put off funding their retirement until after all their children have finished college and the kids have moved away. They then find out that now there is no money left over for retirement. There are actually many ways to save for education in separate buckets. Just like retirement, there are ways to auto save for school as well. Two great options are through 529 savings plans and also life insurance (for yourself). Life insurance can hold some great advantages for both you and the student. 529 plans work just like a retirement plan and hold some great tax advantages, but the way they save and grow is no different.

If you truly want to fund your children's education, have them look into getting as much scholarship help as they can. Look into less expensive state schools and maybe require that the child take out a small loan to help alleviate the cost. I have fully paid for the education of all my kids, but decided to make each one take out a small student loan to help pay for it. I wanted them to have some "skin in the game." When they graduate they will have to work hard and pay the loan back. This will give them an incentive to perform well in school, find good-paying jobs and also help them appreciate living debt-free once those bills are paid. This way they won't get themselves caught up in even more serious problems such as credit card debt.

A good resource to find out how much college may cost you in the future is http://www.finaid.org/calculators/costprojector.phtml

Memories & Opportunities – Funds

Some of the greatest experiences I've had are taking my family to different cities to watch NFL and NHL games. I'm originally from Chicago, so watching the Bears and Blackhawks with my family is a blast. We even drove up to Salt Lake City during the Olympics, went to a hockey game and I actually caught a puck during the game. My grown kids still talk about that hockey game to this day.

We also set aside money every year for our family vacation. Just last year I took my family to Italy. My father was an Italian immigrant and I took the opportunity to show my family the small town where my father grew up. Those memories are some of the greatest of my life.

"All work and no play makes Jack a dull boy." You need to have fun! I like to reward myself when I get to certain milestones in my financial life. I sacrificed for many years trying to save money. We lived in an apartment home, worked multiple jobs, drove older cars that barely ran and saved money while I built my business.

Opportunities that I've been able to invest in have taken our investment portfolio to the next level. Subway restaurant ownership, land deals, companies I have invested in....None of these would have been possible without preparing years ahead of time and having the money ready to invest when the opportunities presented themselves.

Living Longer After All

Living longer is a good problem to have. There's a fun website called www.livingto100.com. On this site, you can put in your health status and what your lifestyle is, and it will then give you an approximate age of how long you're going to live. According to the website, I'm going to live well into my 90s.

Whether I retire at age 60 or 65, I'll need to have enough money to sustain myself into my 90s. Twenty one years is the average time a person in the U.S. spends in retirement. But savings are only lasting 14 years, and then it's completely depleted. It leaves a shortfall on average of seven years, which is scary. What some people don't realize is that they need to adjust their goals.

How many times do we see people who are still working in their 70s or 80s? I'd like to think they are working because they want to, but when I stop and talk to them, they are there because they have to be, because they can't live on Social Security alone.

What is the average amount Social Security pays today? It's between $1,500 a month and about $2,400 a month, depending on how much you put in over the years. Imagine working so long only to find out you've come to the end before you even wanted to be there? You don't want to be the person looking back, wishing you had made a plan ahead of time.

Even with all these factors and complications of life, it can still be easy to make a plan in a few minutes to protect the rest of your life. We have noted many different, quick fixes that can get you moving in the right direction. By saving automatically, putting insurance into place and having fun, you will be on the right track.

5 Mistakes to Avoid

MISTAKE #1: Emotion

Probably the biggest mistake I see is when people get too emotional about investing. When the market is going up, they contribute like crazy into their retirement plans because they feel good emotionally. When the market goes down, they panic, they get nervous, and they pull out of the market. They are buying high and then selling low and they become emotional about investing.

CORRECTION #1: Dollar Cost Averaging

By saving money directly from your paycheck into an investment account every two weeks, you're doing what's called Dollar Cost Averaging. This means whether the market is up or down, you are buying shares with a set amount of money, although obviously less when the market is down. Dollar Cost Averaging is a really effective way to invest in the market, because people just cannot time the market. Even the greatest investors in the world cannot time the market.

Dalbar did a study looking at the average of the market and also how investors reacted. As investors, we all tend to become emotional about investing. If you remember back in 2006 and 2007, home prices were going through the roof, the stock market was extremely high and people felt good so they were investing money at that point. When the market crashed in '08, people didn't feel good. They had just lost 50% of their 401k so they pulled the money out, went to cash and stopped contributing. Instead of buying low and selling high, they were buying high and selling low, which is the opposite of what you want to do. The Dalbar study found that over a 20 year period, the S&P 500 (a stock market index of 500 large companies in the U.S.) did 8.2%. The average investor had a return of 4.25%. Basically, the average investor, investing emotionally, had a return half that of how the market performed.

By automating your investments and being disciplined about investing, it will become a habit. Then you will not have a chance to second guess yourself. Putting it on autopilot takes all the debate off the table.

MISTAKE #2: Timing

The next biggest mistake is probably that of timing, "Let's do this next year. Let's do this when I get a raise or pay off our debt," and unfortunately, that day never comes. People are constantly putting off starting their retirement savings. That's a big mistake!

CORRECTION #2: Start Early, Start Now

If at 25 years of age, you decide to wait until you are age 30 to start investing, you would have to save about 35% more. Let's say for example, you save $300 a month at age 25. You will have $1 million at 8% interest by age 65 with this monthly investment. If you wait until you are 30, you would have to save

$466 a month to hit the same goal of $1 million. This is due to the loss of five years of compounding interest. That's a big difference!

Now if you decide to wait until you are 55, then to reach the $1 million by 65, you would have to save $5,550 a month!!

Reference pages 14 and 15 for graphs showing how timing and compound interest can affect the final value of your retirement savings.

MISTAKE #3: Adjustments

Another big mistake is being too conservative about investing. If you are putting money into a savings account or money market, on average, you can expect to earn only 1% or less. With inflation at 3%, you are automatically losing 2% or MORE every year. In other words, if a quart of milk costs $2 today, next year it could cost $2.06. But the $2 you saved last year now has a value of $2.02. In one year, you have lost 4 cents!

CORRECTION #3:
Aggressive vs. Conservative Investing

So while you can set your account to deposit and invest money on a monthly or bi-weekly basis, adjustments to the overall investment mix are suggested to be done on a yearly basis. Another option would be a Target Date Fund. These are typically found in your 401k, IRA and Roth IRA accounts. What a Target Date Fund says is, "Okay, if you're going to retire 30 years from now (2015), go out and find a fund with a target-date of 2045." This target date is in reference to your retirement year. That fund will be heavier in stocks initially, making it more aggressive and riskier. This in turn gives the advantage of greater initial returns. That takes all the guessing out of your retirement investing.

Target Date Funds are a great option for most to start with. For others, I recommend looking into investment options. This allows you to individualize the account, investing with different rates of risk and diversification than what a Target Date Fund would provide.

MISTAKE #4: Effect of Taxes

Taxes are just a way of life it seems, but many forget to take the effect of taxes into their retirement planning. Retirement income and placement is a strategy in itself.

CORRECTION #4: Deferment options

You need to plan for retirement income and spending now. You can put off paying taxes on a 401k or an IRA. Then, when you pull the money out, you are taxed as ordinary income. Part of the whole mindset to seeing your future in retirement is doing a budget for that future. Where do you want to live? How often do you want to travel? How much do you think you're going to spend in retirement?

There is an art to pulling money out for retirement so that you can place yourself in a lower tax bracket. I like putting my money into Roth retirement and other tax free accounts. That means I pay taxes on the money before I put it away. So when I retire, I don't pay taxes on the money I pull out. I would love to move to a high tax state like California or New York. They are great places to live, but horrible places to pay taxes.

MISTAKE #5: Not Enough Insurance

Another big mistake is being properly insured, whether that is life insurance, disability insurance or both. One out of four people become disabled at some point during their working life. Even a short period of disability can have dramatic and long lasting effects.

CORRECTION #5:
Planning for the worst case scenario

Putting $200 into your 401k every two weeks is wonderful and will have a long-term benefit for you and your family. However, if something were to happen to you a month later, as the sole income earner, money will no longer be saved. And your family will be left with the $400 saved.

Life insurance will provide for your family should something happen to you. Disability (short-term and long-term) insurance will help cover expenses for as long as you are unable to work. Long-term care insurance helps take the burden off nursing home care in the future.

20 Minutes = Sleep Better Tonight

What does 20 minutes look like?

- Review of your current retirement investment options at work
- Rundown of your current expenses and debt- develop a strategy to eliminate debt and reduce expenses
- Discuss your goals for retirement, college education funding, and experiences you want to have
- Leave with exact numbers you'll need to invest monthly to hit those goals and fund your buckets. Meaning- execute your plan
- Meet at least 2 times per year to make sure you're on track

Your Personal Plan

Here's How to Get Your Financial Plan Created and in Place in Just 20 Minutes...

When it comes to saving for retirement, you are probably overwhelmed with the question of whether to invest or whether to pay off debt first. The confusing part is not knowing the easy ways you can maximize your money and make it work for you.

In just 20 minutes we will direct you and clear up your confusion to get you started in the right direction.

Step 1: Visit www.20MinutePlan.com and sign up for your free 20 Minutes.

Step 2: Spend 20 minutes with a financial planner and get a clear idea of how to achieve your goals.

Step 3: Follow your plan. Get access to support and tools as you progress with your financial future.

Most people are not aware of the simple ways to plan for retirement and think it takes a lot of time. It really doesn't! We'll show you how and create your roadmap to success.

Now you can get your financial plan outlined and in place in as little as 20 Minutes.

Get started today, go to www.20MinutePlan.com now!

About the Author

Phil Randazzo is a second generation Sicilian who learned early on from his father that this country offers the greatest opportunities in the world. At a young age, Phil quickly learned the value of hard work. From clearing tables at his father's restaurants to working three summer jobs from age fifteen until graduating college, he realized he wanted to work for himself.

Starting his first company at age twenty-four, to make ends meet, he delivered newspapers at night, helped write parole and probation reports nights and weekends, and sold benefits to companies with 100 percent commissions during the day.

His time is currently being spent writing, consulting, and developing a national entrepreneurship and coaching program called American Dream U, held at military bases around the country. www.AmericanDreamU.org is a nonprofit organization that assists the military transitioning into civilian life. The program is designed to help Soldiers, Airmen, Sailors, Marines, and Coast Guard personnel obtain their dream jobs or start their own businesses. The program is taught by some of the world's best and most successful entrepreneurs.

Phil was given the key to the City of Las Vegas in March of 2003 by Mayor Oscar Goodman. He is actively involved in the Las Vegas community, serving on the Advisory Board for the YMCA of Southern Nevada and the Nevada Military Support Alliance. Recently, Mr. Randazzo was commissioned by Governor Brian Sandoval as a member of the Veterans Services Commission.

Phil attended Ball State University and received his MBA from University of Phoenix. He lives in Las Vegas with his wife, Jennifer, of over twenty years, and his three college-age children, Philip, attending and playing basketball at Elmhurst College in Chicago, Megan, attending UCLA, and Joseph, attending and playing basketball at the University of Puget Sound in Tacoma, Washington.